Geo Gems 2

CreativeColoringBooksForAdults.com

MandaLove Press

Hours of coloring fun inside ...

Geo Gems Volume Two is a huge book of 50 mandala designs created using geometric shapes such as circle, square, polygon, star, and rectangle. Packed within these pages are hours of creative fun for the entire family.

Geo Gems Volume Two is filled with original, one-of-a-kind coloring patterns ranging from simple and easy to complex. Based on geometric patterns found in nature and math class, our coloring book is a great art and teaching resource for the home schooler or tutor.

With 50 designs to choose from, each member of the family can easily find a mandala that sparks their imagination and inspires their inner artist.

Geo Gems Volume Two is the second coloring book in our geometric series – be sure and collect them all! Each coloring book is unique, and filled with original designs that are not repeated in other books in the series.

The mandala designs in **Geo Gems Volume Two** are printed one to a page, but markers can bleed through even the best paper. Two blotter pages have been added to the back of the book for you to use to keep your artwork pristine.

Free coloring pages ...

Subscribe to our newsletter today and we'll send you a free bonus set of mandalas to color. You'll also have a chance to win a brand new coloring book! We choose a new winner every month:
http://CreativeColoringBooksForAdults.SubscribeMeNow.com/

Join us on Facebook and you'll have access to free coloring pages and more chances to win free coloring supplies and coloring books:
https://www.Facebook.com/CreativeColoringBooks

Look for our coloring books on Amazon and at your local bookstore!

Thank you for supporting independent artists!

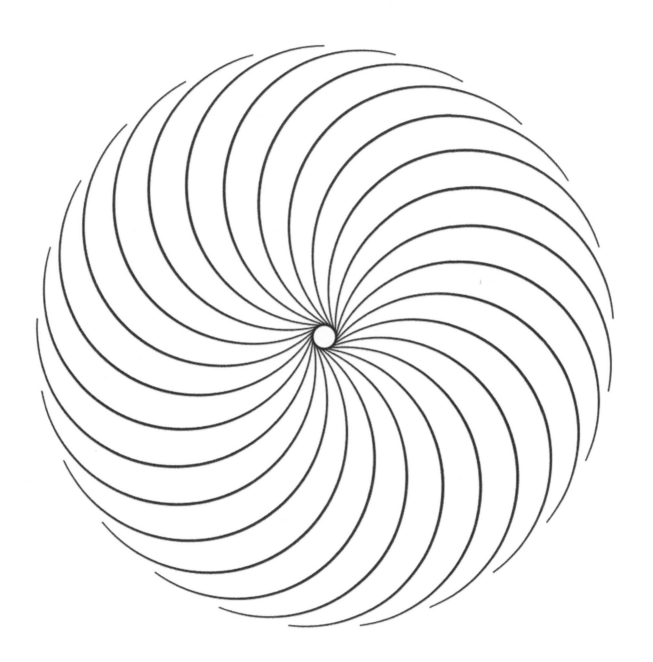

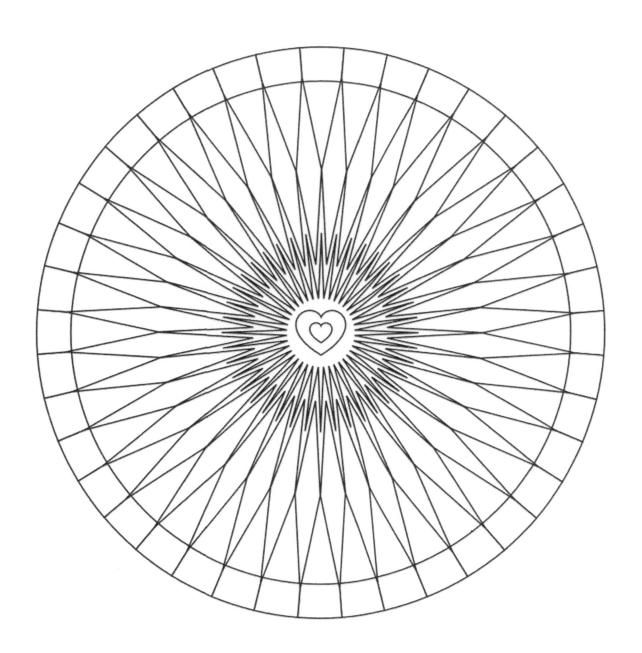

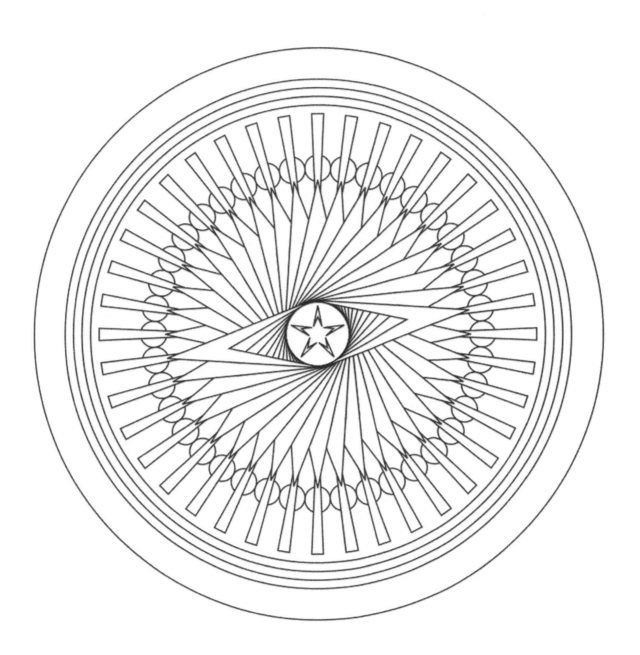

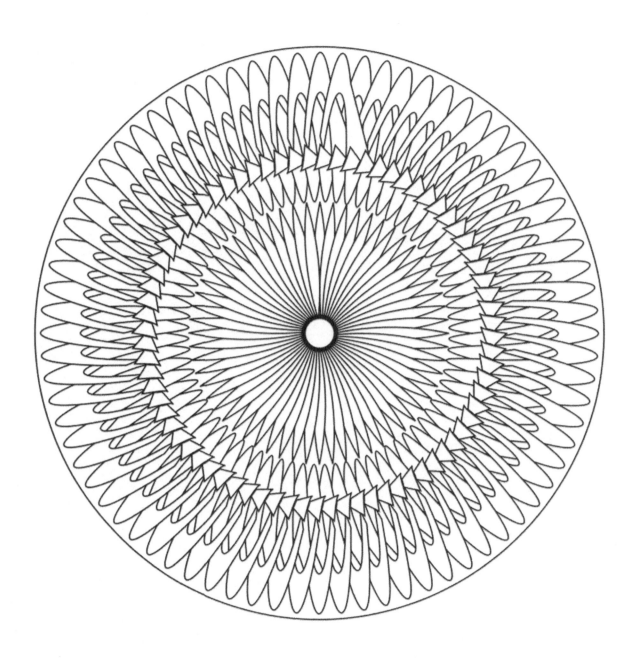

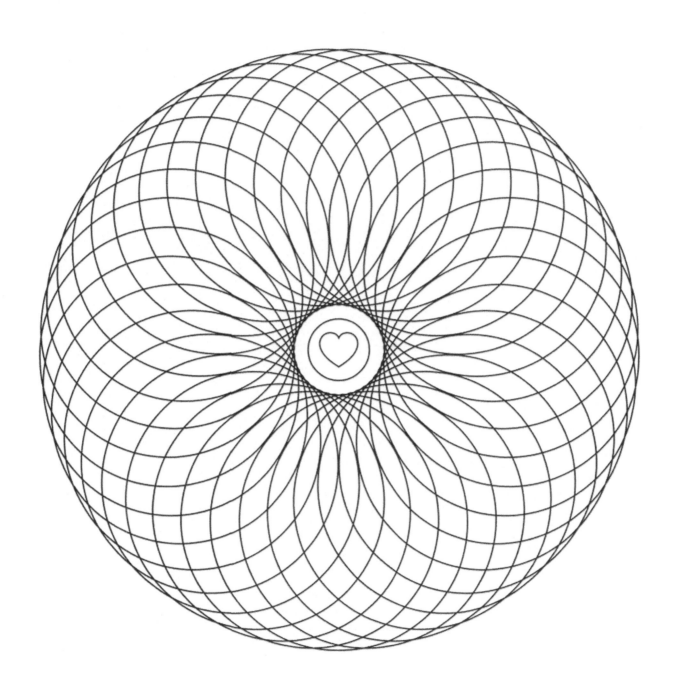

Notes

Notes

Blotter Page

Two blotter pages have been included for your convenience. Remove one or both and use them as a barrier between the page you are coloring and the next. The designs in this book have been printed on one side of the page, but markers often bleed through even the best paper. To keep your art work pristine as you color and create, use another piece of paper as a buffer between the pages of this book, or use a thin piece of cardboard (cut one side from a cereal box, or use the thin cardboard insert that is found inside a new shirt)

Blotter Page

Two blotter pages have been included for your convenience. Remove one or both and use them as a barrier between the page you are coloring and the next. The designs in this book have been printed on one side of the page, but markers often bleed through even the best paper. To keep your art work pristine as you color and create, use another piece of paper as a buffer between the pages of this book, or use a thin piece of cardboard (cut one side from a cereal box, or use the thin cardboard insert that is found inside a new shirt)